The GEEZER'S GUIDE to ADVENTURE

Donald J. Hurzeler

The GEEZER'S GUIDE to ADVENTURE

The Geezer's Guide to Adventure

By Donald J. Hurzeler

First Edition

Published by
Kua Bay Publishing LLC

Paperback ISBN: 979-8-9857875-5-9

Hardcover ISBN: 979-8-9857875-6-6

I dedicate this book to our grandkids, Ava Stanczak, Nathan Stanczak, Sam Hurzeler, Zach Hurzeler, and Julia Hurzeler.

When our grandkids turn twelve, we take them anywhere they want to go in the world, first-class, for up to a month. So far, we have traveled with Ava to Europe, Nathan to Australia, and Sam to Korea and Japan. Next up is Zach. Jules is much younger, and we will do our best to hang on so we can enjoy a great trip with her too. Or, perhaps, we can talk her into an afternoon at the local Walmart as we will be in our mideighties by then.

Our grandkids are the extension of ourselves into the future...much of which we will not be around to see. So, we want them to know us...to know how much we love them...to see us as vigorous older versions of themselves, and to have the curiosity and confidence to go see the world.

Thank God for grandkids. We ended up with five we love and respect.

Contents

Introduction to Adventure

So, I am standing in a back alley by myself, somewhere along the Nile River in Egypt, with a fully grown GIANT king cobra draped around my shoulders. It was at that moment that I realized that I had been lied to...by everyone. Retirement was not going to be boring and "careful."

I realized that retirement was going to be exactly what *I* decided it would be...and I decided it would be the greatest adventure of my life. Make that...our lives. My wife of over fifty-five years, Linda, joined me in this decision. We were not going to just fade away. We were determined to test our limits, explore the things that had previously scared us, and see the world. Retirement was going to absolutely rock! It was the second-best decision of my life, with the first best being the decision to marry Linda.

Society had told us that retirement was just a steady decline into old age and oblivion. To be fair, part of that is true: We *will* get old and there *will* be an end to the fun. But instead of inspiring us all with the idea that some of the best years of our lives are directly in front of us at retirement, things seem stacked up to discourage us—to scare us that we will run out of money, have a stroke on our first trip to France, be taken advantage of by the wily youngsters that roam the streets of the world or, heaven forbid, get in the way of the young people who are actually doing something with their lives. **What a heaping crock!** Retirement is our time to really enjoy our FREEDOM and to explore our dreams.

This book is designed to INSPIRE you to put big-time adventure into your retirement years, to give you the tools to make that happen safely and economically, and to give you the confidence that you can make your life the best life that you can imagine.

I hate pie-in-the-sky talk and writing about things that sound good but cannot actually be done by normal human beings. This book is about reality. It's about things you can do whether you are rich or poor, in good health or not, single or married, adventuresome or timid.

You can shape your retirement life to include a healthy dose of adventure *if you want to*. My opinion is, why not give it a good try and then decide?

I

How I Ended Up with That Giant King Cobra Draped Around My Shoulders in a Back Alley in Egypt

Linda and I retired when I was sixty-one. To be honest, I retired a bit early because I had topped out in my career and had just recovered from a nasty bout of cancer. Linda had a cancer scare, as well. We were otherwise in good shape and financially secure.

I recognize that we all arrive at our senior years in different states of being. Some of us are healthy...others are fully disabled. A few are wealthy and completely secure money-wise. But most of us are worried whether we will have enough money to last us to the end. And some of us are just plain broke.

But no matter what our condition, there is fun to be had out there in our geezer years...big fun and wonderful adventures. But that fun and those adventures are unlikely to come find us so we are going to have to go find them. And so, my wife and I set out early in our retirement to see if we could pinpoint the things we had only dreamed of up to this point.

Linda and I had been just about everywhere before we retired. But, in my case, visiting Belgium might have meant landing at the airport, going to an airline club for a meeting, and then getting back on the plane and flying home because it was a work trip. Not much of a way to enjoy a country and see what it has to offer. So, we decided to explore the half dozen or so countries that most interested us and do so in long-form—we would go to each country for a month.

First up was Australia.

Australia was a perfect, and relatively safe, place to start. They speak something close to English, the food and water treated us well, and there were lots of things to see and do. We loved our month there.

Next up was Egypt.

We visited Egypt in late 2009, as tensions were rising toward an uprising that began in 2010. By 2011, that uprising turned into a revolution.

In late 2009, Egypt was a scary place for people from the United States. As one local told us when he learned that's where we were from—"Danger, danger, danger!" But we knew that ahead of time and took precautions. We dressed as locals, were driven around in a nondescript car, stayed away from large gatherings and tour vehicles, and had armed security with us at all times. Linda and I are risk-takers, but we are not foolish. We stacked the odds heavily in our favor and got along fine.

Until Linda got as sick as I have ever seen a person get. During the day or so that she was down for the count, she insisted that I explore a town along the Nile that we were scheduled to see while she stayed in the hotel and recovered. So, I headed off with my security guy.

This place I visited was not a big town. It was a small town that had antiquities to visit and a lot of places for tourists to spend a few dollars. At some point, my security guy told me to stay still while he ran off to get some cigarettes. I do not do still well. I wandered into an alley, came upon two teenagers handling the biggest snake I had ever seen and walked over to see what was going on.

The kids did not speak English, and my Arabic was poor at the time (not that it has improved since then). We did some hand signaling and it became apparent that they would let me put the big harmless snake around my shoulders for just two dollars. Bargain. I gave them the money and they placed the huge snake over my shoulders with its tail on the ground on one side and its head moving around on the ground on the other. I was stoked.

Suddenly, I see a man charging toward me. It was my security guard. He seemed in a panic. What could be wrong? He started yelling at me about the snake. I informed him that it was just a harmless snake and not to worry. But he yelled at the kids, and they took the snake and ran off. Turns out it was not a harmless snake; it was a king cobra that they were taking to the local venom extraction center to be milked for its venom.

That did it. That changed my mind forever about risk. Those kids knew that snake was used to being handled and was safe. Never, ever, in my entire life had I thought I might encounter, much less wear a king cobra. But I did, and I survived the experience. So, while the security guard fumed at me, I smiled to myself and quietly wondered what else I might be able to survive if I stacked the odds in my favor and got some expert help. And that stacking of odds and getting help is the key to my...and your...adding big-time adventure to your life.

2

A Game Plan for Becoming Adventurous in Our Senior Years

I am not an advocate of doing stupid things. That is not to say that I have not taken some stupid risks—that snake was one and swimming with saltwater crocodiles comes to mind as another. However, I try not to take risks lightly. And, I have a plan for taking on new risks.

Here is my plan...

I start off small and build from there.

I learn to be comfortable in the ocean around eels, jellyfish, dolphins, and mantas...really comfortable...before I step up the adventure to include reef sharks and eventually big scary sharks. I do not start off jumping into the water with a tiger shark to see what will happen.

I study the risk before I act.

I will read up on animal or fish behavior, how to survive at high altitude, or whatever the planned adventure might be. I also check out similar adventures on YouTube. I try to know what I am getting into so I can plan for the hard parts.

I train for the adventure.

Before I jump in with sharks, I take time to build my swimming skills and confidence in the water using big swim fins, a face mask, and a snorkel. I don't want it to all be new at the same time. One step at a time wins the day. Same with hiking, climbing, or any other type of physical adventure. That's quite different from the Nike slogan, "Just Do It." My slogan is "Get ready and then do it."

I work with a coach or security person.

If you see me doing something that most people would consider dangerous, look around and you will find an expert nearby. I don't hike out to running lava by myself. I do not go into big wave situations without expert big wave people around me. I would never drape a big snake over my shoulders without the security of TWO teenage kids I had never met assuring me through sign language that it was safe. I am prone to occasional stupidity, but, in general, I have an expert nearby watching out for my safety.

can visit most national parks at night for free. Many have no gates and no restrictions about visiting at night. All also have some days a year you can visit for free. As a result, I can hike a different trail each week for life without repeating any. Lots and lots of adventures are out there for people without any money at all. Heck, in Hawaii, even the bus is free...you can explore this whole fabulous island for free every single day.

I am absolutely clear on the fact that lack of resources, and physical and mental limitations, can get in the way of adventure in our old age...in a significant way. However, please go back to my main theme here: What *can* you do? Do what you can—you are not excluded from the fun zone. In fact, I think you will find yourself very much welcome there.

For people lucky enough to live in urban areas, there are art, science, and natural history museums that usually offer free admission some days of the week; free public concerts and movies; art galleries that are open to everyone; parks and gardens created by top-notch landscape designers; senior centers that offer low-cost classes, presentations about topics that could open up new possibilities for you; book and poetry readings; downtown shopping areas with myriad stores and a coffee shop on every block; public libraries; and informal meetings for specific interest groups. Check out your local paper and community bulletin boards on the internet such as Nextdoor, and you'll probably find something new to do every day.

4

Adventures for Single Seniors

I would never have thought to mention this topic a decade ago, but I am seeing more and more contemporaries who have lost their spouse or partner. I also have a few friends who never chose to marry, and they have told me that being single gets in the way of their wish to travel.

I travel enough to know about this thing called "the single supplement." What that means is that if you are traveling alone and need a room for yourself, you are going to pay more for that room than you would if you were traveling with a companion and sharing a room. You can frame that up in your head to feel that you are unfairly being charged more to travel just because you are single, *or* you can frame it up to realize you are traveling for a heck of a lot less money than you would be paying if you were traveling in company and paying for two. But either way, I do understand it is a factor that is irritating as heck.

Of course, there is a simple solution...travel with a friend you are willing to room with on the road or ask a tour operator to team you up with another single. Not perfect, perhaps, but that strategy will save some money.

The real disadvantage of traveling single is that it is often easier and potentially more fun to travel with a loved one...someone you know completely and trust. Someone whose snoring you are used to.

Traveling solo can be a challenge but I refer you back to my main theme: What *can* you do?" For starters, you can find a way. Heck, you might even find a new partner. Or you might discover that you thoroughly enjoy the freedom and adventure of traveling alone...you never know.

5

The National Park Pass...Best Investment of My Life

I love our national parks...love them. And if you have reached the age of sixty-two, you can enjoy them for just $20 a year or $80 for a lifetime with an America the Beautiful national parks and federal recreational lands pass.

At the time I got my lifetime senior pass, the fee was either $10 or $25...can't remember. But I do remember that I got the cost of it back the very first time I used it. That pass and your driver's license can get you into over 2,000 national parks, national monuments, and other federal recreation sites...along with a carload of up to four people...at no cost past the original $20 annual or lifetime fee of $80 ...repeatedly. However, even with a pass, you may need a timed reservation for some high-traffic sites. Check https://home.nps.gov/planyourvisit/passes.htm for information.

So, national parks and the like are not totally free. But they can be accessed by seniors, wealthy or not, for the price of the pass and the gas. And they are all over the country.

We have two national parks near us. A national historical park... The City of Refuge or Pu'uhonua O Honaunau, is located about fifteen minutes from our home on the Big Island of Hawai'i. I mention it because it is next to one of the great snorkeling and dive spots on this island, Two Step. I show my pass, park in the lot for free, and walk the short distance to the Two Step. The parking lot is safe and supervised, while the surrounding area is either congested with heavy parking, not completely safe, or you have to pay for your parking. My national parks pass makes parking easy...and the park itself is great to visit.

Hawai'i Volcanoes National Park is an hour-and-a-half drive from our house. We have worn out our senior pass while visiting that park hundreds of times. We do a lot of photography there, but also a lot of hiking...leaving the car in a safe area of the park where we can be quite sure it will still be there when we return.

In addition, there are six days each year when all national parks are open for free, pass or no pass. Which leaves only two hurdles...the gas or electricity to get to a national park and your own physical or mental ability to access the park.

Going back to my theme of What *can* you do?—think in terms of teaming up with others who are short on money and going in together to cut your costs down by half or more. In some cases, public transportation may get you to the gate, and some parks have transportation systems within the park. You can do this!

As for disabilities...I hear you...limited mobility and other constraints are going to restrict your access for sure. However, the parks I have visited have made significant efforts to be inclusive and to provide services and facilities for those who face challenges. Again... What *can* you do? I think the answer is *a lot*.

Searching the internet, taking a book on national parks out of the library, or asking friends for suggestions will leave you with a long list of places that interest you. I often look at maps and find little-known national monuments, and the like, that are not the big-time national parks, but generally have one or more interesting aspects. For example, I was just in Arizona for business. I had one extra day so I rented a car and went to Montezuma Castle National Monument. I got in for free, though there was the rental car expense and the gas. And I got there when it opened, and when no one else had arrived yet.

Montezuma Castle is kind of a one-trick pony...a massive cliff dwelling halfway up a sheer rock formation. If you walk along the bottom of the cliff and look up...it will blow you mind. How they built that structure and lived there for centuries...amazing! I spent less than an hour and not one cent. I took lots of photos. It was a great use of my time. Here is a photo of the dwellings I took with my cell phone.

I then ventured on to one of my favorite national parks, Petrified Forest National Park near the border of Arizona and New Mexico. I got in for free, spent all day driving, looking at petroglyphs, hiking, and taking a few hundred photos...and spent only $2.50 for a snack on the way out. However, I do love petrified wood, so I always stop *outside* the gates of the park and *buy* some...seems they take a very dim view of your collecting the petrified wood on your own. I think I bought too much on this trip.

Actually, that's not my car. I only bought 700 pounds of petrified wood to ship back to Hawaii...seriously. This car is parked permanently in the parking lot of the Petrified Forest Gift Shop and RV Park...and it always makes me smile. One more tip: they do have hours that they are closed so make sure to check their schedule.

6

Not All National Parks Are Created Equal

This is a legendary story in my family and a painful one for me.

I found a national monument on a map back when we still had young kids. We were on a vacation that took us to Wyoming and the Dakotas...to places like Mount Rushmore and Devils Tower National Monument. Back in those days, we navigated by paper maps. I went over those maps with a magnifying glass looking for fun things to visit. I found one...Agate Fossil Beds National Monument.

Look up Agate Fossil Beds National Park. It is in the middle of nowhere in northwest Nebraska. We started the day in the Badlands of South Dakota and then I surprised the family with this great side trip to Agate Fossil Beds National Monument. Surprised is not the perfect word here...let's settle on aggravated... I aggravated them. The trip was a big mistake.

The park is way off the beaten path. It was summer, hot and dusty. There was nothing to see during the hours it took to get there. I knew I was in trouble when I stopped at a small store that, according to the map, was within five miles of the national monument. I asked the young clerk how much further to the fossil beds. She had never heard of it. I asked her how long she had lived in the area. Her response: "All my life." Uh oh.

This was decades ago, and things may have changed. But at the time we visited Agate Fossil Beds National Monument, it consisted of a mobile-home-looking structure, one park ranger (who looked parched and was probably thinking he had made a poor career choice), a dirt parking lot, and a dusty semi-asphalt trail out into the prairie. The ranger was not much of a talker, but he pointed to the trail and off we went.

Did you know that Nebraska has rattlesnakes on the prairie in the summer? We did not. We saw and heard a few. That was not a plus for this mission.

When we got to the site, it consisted of a bunch of holes in the ground and pictures of the long-ago museum people removing said fossils from the ground to take back east to their museum. That was all.

This photo of my young (at the time) daughter, Stephanie, sums up the day. Look carefully at her beautiful and scornful face.

I guess the point is...know before you go. Some national parks and monuments are in very remote places, can be a one-trick (or no-trick) pony, and may not be worth the effort.

I am now seventy-seven and the Agate Fossil Beds National Monument trip haunts me to this day. You may want to scratch it off your bucket list.

7

And Some National Parks Were Made in Heaven

You probably already know this list or have your own. This is not a book on national parks, but there are a few that are spectacular, and you should try to see at least one of them. I will leave the research to you, but here is a good starter list...

- Yellowstone (in several states, but mostly Wyoming)
- Zion (Utah)
- Bryce (Utah)
- Grand Canyon (Arizona)
- Petrified Forest (Arizona)
- Glacier (Montana)
- Volcanoes (Hawai'i)
- Arches (Utah)
- Acadia (Maine)
- Carlsbad Caverns (New Mexico)
- Death Valley (California)
- Denali (Alaska)
- Everglades (Florida)

- Great Smoky Mountains (North Carolina and Tennessee)
- Mesa Verde (Colorado)
- Mt. Rainier (Washington)
- Sequoia (California)
- Yosemite (California)
- Rocky Mountains (Colorado)
- Indiana Dunes (Indiana)

There are more than sixty national parks in the United States and some in our territories, including the US Virgin Islands and Samoa.

And just about every one of the 111 countries that we have visited has its own national park system. You can easily spend a lifetime exploring them for very little cost other than the time and expense of the travel—which can be considerable.

I love our national parks.

8

Other Places to Go in the USA

I am still trying to add to the "What *can* you do?" list, thinking about things that almost anyone can do for little money.

As an example, Linda and I have driven between Page, Arizona—one of the great small towns in America near slot canyons, Native American land, Horseshoe Bend, the Colorado River, and the magnificent Glen Canyon Dam area—and Zion National Park...maybe a dozen times so far. We always passed the turnoff to Coral Pink Sand Dunes State Park in Utah. It sounded interesting, but it was a considerable drive off the main road, so we just kept going to Zion.

One day we decided to see what was in that state park. What is there are miles of sand dunes—pink, beautiful, remote—profound solitude, and the chance that you might see some maniac in a dune buggy trying to see if they can make that vehicle fly. We loved it...well worth the effort and we have been back twice since the initial trip.

Now this may cause you concern for my sanity, but keep in mind that I am a photographer and storyteller, which may explain the following.

I love to explore big cities, New York City being my favorite, Washington, DC coming in second, and Boston third. I love to walk the streets, ride public transportation, see the people, look in the stores, go to the museums, and enjoy the street entertainment.

I have seen a monkey loose inside a subway car late at night in New York. Witnessed several gun fights from a distance—and from behind a park bench— run into the musician Sting...just him and me... at the base of the World Trade Tower at about one in the morning, gone to amazing parades—the Pride March, the National Puerto Rican Day Parade, the Macy's Thanksgiving Day Parade, and the St. Patrick's Day Parade—and been there for the dropping of the ball at midnight on New Year's Eve in Times Square. All free...all fun...all adventuresome...just enough danger to keep you alert. I also went to several Central Park concerts for free...one with Garth Brooks that had over a million people attending.

Give me a day and I can either walk a city and have a good time or pick a central spot to just sit and watch humanity go by. Either way, it will be a day well spent and cost me next to nothing.

I like fishing for free—some states require a license, but Hawai'i does not—from piers, shorelines, rivers, boats, and lakes. An odd recent development is that I have taken so many photos of fish that I think of them as my friends, and I've lost some of my desire to catch them. Trout, however, does not enjoy that status. I am happy to eat trout day in and day out.

I like being part of BIG events, even if I do not attend them. I can be happy doing a tailgate lunch near a big event, even if I do not attend because it's sold out. I've stood outside arenas with a radio and some friends and listened to sold-out events. I like the energy and the feeling of belonging. The point is—I try to find ways to do things...even if it is not perfect.

If you can hike and are willing to explore backcountry, you can do so in most places for free—other than the expense to get there—and find lost civilizations...cliff dwellings, petroglyphs, pottery shards (please leave everything where you found it).

Sometimes on those long hikes, you find *yourself* out there. I find hikes to be a great way to explore my own thoughts.

Activities that might sound nerdy but grow on you include bird watching. Again, no cost. You can do it for a lifetime and never see all the varieties. I love it, but I avoid the competitive birders who drive me nuts with their lists and extreme knowledge of my bird friends. I am more of a I-saw-a-red-bird-and-a-blue-one kind of a guy.

Here is another nerdy one…rock collecting. Before you start your collection, try to check out the *free* (some require admission, but focus on the free ones first) annual Tucson Gem and Mineral Show in January and February. It will astonish you. The entire town is selling rocks…from pieces of quartz to really fancy stuff. I have learned to ask where the rocks are collected and then I go find them myself, at least those that come from the United States. The show is very international.

If you do go to that show, you can just look for free and do so for days on end. If you plan to buy, bring cash and negotiate hard—you can get fabulous prices and great specimens to collect dust in your home for years to come. I think of those rocks as my kids' inheritance. I am working hard to spend whatever money I have turning dollars into rocks wherever possible.

I almost forgot to mention the seasons. I also travel a lot to explore the seasons and what they have to offer. They include fall colors on the East Coast and in the Rockies; snow in Yellowstone in the heart of winter; big waves on the North Shore of Oahu in the winter; holiday window shopping in Chicago or New York City; small town Fourth of July parades and fireworks in places like Barrington, Illinois; and The New Orleans Jazz & Heritage Festival.

One special note: Those who live anywhere where there is warm water during all or parts of the year and where conditions are relatively safe can go to a thrift store and find a swim mask, snorkel, and fins for next to nothing.

We chose to retire in Hawai'i, in large part, for two reasons. We wanted to be able to walk, run, hike outside virtually every day of the year for free, and we wanted to snorkel in a warm clear ocean every day of the year for free. We also wanted there to be enough variety in our snorkels and hikes to make it interesting for the rest of our lives. Well...mission accomplished...we found what we were looking for. We had to move from the comfort of our Chicago home to do it. But we did and never looked back. One of the great decisions of our lives.

And one does not have to be rich to live in Hawai'i. One of my great friends, a guy I grew up with in California who is my age lives here and he is stone cold broke. He lives here happily, but very simply. I think his place is only 150 square feet, does not have solid walls (more like a tent), has no utilities and he has had to move away from lava flows three times. I doubt he would tell you it is perfect, but it accommodates the lifestyle he wants, and fits with his lack of finances. He seems very happy, content, and productive.

I've been more financially fortunate in life, but I am equally happy with my broke friend. We both do a few things to make the finances easier: we both write and get paid for our writing, work a bit when we want, barter for things we need, and grow some of our own food. It takes some thought, but you can make the finances work anywhere you choose to live. Sounds daunting, I know, but it all works out.

I will exclude the Hamptons and Beverly Hills from the statement above.

And just to remind you—I am now seventy-seven—and for the first time in my life I am sure that I will not outlive my money. It won't even be close. We all have that fear, but that is what it is...fear. Take good care of whatever finances you have, and you too will make it to the finish line with money in the bank.

Always Have Something to Look Forward to in the Not-Too-Distant Future

Whether you are rich, poor, or in between, we geezers need to always have something out there on the horizon to look forward to. I strongly believe that. Those future events pull us through the difficult days that show up during our senior years and keep us thinking positively. I promise you that I will have several things ahead of me on the calendar, deposits paid, and commitments made on the day I die.

I know I will be in Yellowstone in January, Tucson for the Gem and Mineral Show in February, back home in Hawai'i in time to enjoy the whales and big surf before winter is over and experience a summertime of heavy-duty snorkeling and manta trips, and then somewhere else looking for colors in the fall. In addition to lots of visits with friends, old and new, in between. There are birthdays already on the calendar to celebrate with friends. You get the idea...I have a full calendar of things to look forward to in my geezer years.

If that sounds unrealistic for your situation, take some time and an old-fashioned paper calendar, and write out what you know you have ahead in your life...both the obligations and the fun. If you end up short on fun, read the preceding chapters again and give it some thought—there is fun out there to be had for all of us. Fun does not care about your bank balance. Fun cares about your willingness to have fun. It is yours for the grabbing.

My Tricks for Making Travel Nearly Fun and Nearly Affordable

I have traveled first class millions of miles during my career and it was nearly always a pleasant experience. On rare occasions, I got to travel on my company's corporate jet. On my last trip upon retirement, the pilot came to see me before I disembarked. He advised me to look around carefully. I asked why, and what should I notice. He said, "Everything because you will probably never see the inside of a private jet again in your life." He said that in the nicest possible way and as part of a sincere goodbye to me. And I took it as he meant it to be...a joking way of saying goodbye. However, turns out, he was right. I have been retired for sixteen years now and have never made it back onto a private jet. Life changes when you retire.

Within a couple of years of retiring, almost all of my travel perks disappeared. I was not traveling as much and not earning all those bonus points and free miles. At the same time, Linda and I were getting older, carrying more gear with us as we became professional photographers in our retirement (we look like pack mules when we board planes), and feeling the effects of aging. Air travel and hotel stays were becoming more difficult...to the point of discouraging us from traveling. As a generality, I think that the older you get, the more difficult it is to travel, especially on long or big-time adventures.

So...what to do? We talked about it. We did not want to give up our travel life. So, we listed all the travel tricks I had learned over the years to see if we could construct some plan that might make travel easier for us. Here is the list:

First, a word of advice for anyone...front load your senior or retirement years with your most physically demanding travel. For example, visit Machu Picchu when you are first retired. You will find it quite difficult to do it when you are seventy or older. And save the cruise down the Rhine for your old age. Do the easy trips after seventy.

Now, onto our travel ideas...

We have enough lifetime miles that we get bumped to first class whenever there is a seat available, so we look for flights that have lots of seats left in first class and book those usually on Tuesdays or Wednesdays—days when business travelers are not taking all the first-class seats.

We use our travel miles to book business class on overseas trips. When we do not have enough miles to book business class, we use an airline seat consolidator to book those seats for us at WAY below published fares, usually close to economy pricing. I cannot recommend a company for you, as things can change quickly, but we have used Sky Luxe for years with great success.

If we decide to use a travel agent on complex trips, we push that agent hard to get us greatly reduced pricing for business-class seats. If you don't ask, you don't get.

Sometimes we must book economy, but we then work with the airline to get an upgrade. This is done in two ways. Some airlines have a bidding procedure for upgrades...if yours is the highest bid, you get the upgrade for your bid price. We always put in the lowest bid allowed and almost always win the seats.

The second way is to negotiate with the gate agent. Some guidelines for that strategy: Do not show up close to boarding time and give it a try; it will not work. Arrive an hour early and ask if first class is booked full. If it is not, offer them whatever you are willing to pay for that seat right now. I usually start at about $100 a seat. After that, you are in a negotiation and keep at it until you win the seat. Remember, they are going to fill that seat for *no* money with one of their frequent fliers or for *some* money if you buy that seat. You have a better chance of winning than you might think. And that first-class seat comes with access to their first-class lounge—both at that airport and upon arrival.

What does not work is *asking* to be upgraded. That used to work, but today there are so many frequent fliers ahead of you that you have no chance. Forget it.

Credit card benefits can make your trip a lot more pleasant. We chose our credit cards to enhance our travel experience. Our major card gives us access to United Club lounges worldwide. We have a second card that gives us access to basically all the other airline or airport lounges worldwide. This card gives us a gold status for flying, which means early boarding, no luggage fees, economy-plus seating for economy prices, high status at a car rental company, high status at a hotel chain we love, and a bunch of other stuff. It builds up frequent flier miles from your normal purchases and travel purchases quickly and those are good for "free" tickets. The credit card costs us several hundred dollars a year as an annual card fee, but it's well worth it. We never leave any balance on the card for more than a few days because, as with almost all credit cards, the interest rates are outrageous.

By the way, you might be wondering what is inside those airline or airport clubs. Lots of good stuff. Inside you can often get something to eat and drink for no charge, a quieter place to relax before your next flight, and help with travel plans when things like the weather get difficult. Some clubs have showers, sleeping areas, and even massage services. An airline club can save the day, and if it's included in your credit card benefits, why not use it?

We just got back from Japan and the first-class lounge there not only had showers, but the staff also cooked meals to order for us. They also had lockers if we wanted to store our carry-on bags and go out to explore the wonderful shopping available at the airport. Loved it.

We like window seats when there is something to see. We like aisle seats on overnight trips because it's easier to get to the bathroom if needed, and at our age, it is always needed. We like exit rows and bulkhead rows although they are harder to store the items you brought on board. We are also big fans of extra leg room and being able to get out of our seats without bothering those around us.

Another thing my wife and I always do when we travel is pack noise-canceling headphones and sleep masks...and use both. I developed this habit when I was flying for work, and it serves me well today. For example, if I am in a window seat, I board as early as possible, get in my seat, put on my seat belt in a manner that can be seen by flight attendants, put on my face mask and headphones, and fall to sleep. I trained myself to sleep immediately and stay asleep until the plane rotates on takeoff. So, instead of putting up with all the chaos of boarding, I get an extra hour of sleep right at the start of the trip. But I always eventually wake up because I would hate to miss the airline meal.

If you tend to get nervous, anxious, and uptight about travel, make sure to get to the airport early. It is amazing how easy everything works when you arrive an hour or so before boarding.

I also recommend taking an empty bottle through security and filling it with water before you board. If you are in economy, it will be helpful not to have to ask for water—you will have your own.

The best trick up our sleeve for international travel is this.... We are old, retired, and often tired when we go on big-time adventures. So, we try to break the big travel segments into two pieces with a rest day or more in between. For example, to get to Tanzania from Kona, Hawaii, we fly to Los Angeles to Houston to Amsterdam. We then stay at a hotel very near or at the airport in Amsterdam for one to three days and do absolutely nothing other than eat at our favorite restaurant in the world, Lars, for dinner each night. It also helps that we've been to Amsterdam dozens of times, so we have kind of seen it all. After our downtime in Amsterdam, we can then fly to Tanzania well-rested. We do the same on the way back. It's a luxury...absolutely...but we have finally figured out that our health and comfort are worth the extra time and money. And we love the food at Lars.

II

A Half Dozen Adventures to Consider

I gave you my elevator speech on adding adventure to your life and I'll do my best to reinforce it later. I covered my game plan for adding risk and adventure to your geezer years without doing so foolishly. And I gave you my tricks for making the travel part somewhat affordable and somewhat comfortable. The reality is that the transporter room in *Star Trek* is not yet commercially available, so we all must suffer a bit of travel expense and discomfort to make our adventure dreams come true. I hope my suggestions help in that regard.

I am now going to get specific and suggest six travel adventures that we loved that may be worth your consideration to get you out of your normal world and off into the rest of the world. Six great starter trips are Australia, Hawai'i, Yellowstone, Europe, Peru, and Tanzania.

I chose these as starter trips because while a few other places on Earth are probably more interesting, they are harder to get to, harder to navigate, and a bit more foreign. I believe in starting easy and building up to the more exotic or out of our comfort zone. We love China, Japan, Egypt (a must-see when things are safe there), the

Pacific Islands, and the Caribbean. In fact, if it is politically safe at the time you are reading this, I would put Egypt first on your list. However, I have been there when it was dicey, and that is a higher adventure than I would ever recommend.

So, let's start off easy....

#6 Australia

I cannot explain how much I love Australia. As I said, they almost speak English there, the food is recognizable and good, and it is a huge and diverse country. We hit Sydney, Melbourne, Adelaide, Kangaroo Island, Alice Springs, Uluru, Cairns, Port Douglas, Daintree, and the Great Barrier Reef. And we loved them all.

The Great Barrier Reef is a world wonder and vast. We spent about a third of our time on the reef. The best place to launch from is Port Douglas. But make sure to do your research before you book your flights and stays. The ocean around the reefs can host deadly jellyfish at certain times of the year, so you may want to avoid those times. Just to be safe, I wear so-called stinger suits any time I am there as I am not a big fan of any kind of jellyfish stings.

Almost everywhere you go in Australia, you can easily and economically hire a guide...even on the reef. Australia has a lot of deadly creatures, so I hire guides to keep me safe. I have never felt that I was in danger there, but I have seen many things on the land and in the sea that could have presented a danger.

We took our twelve-year-old grandson, Nate, there for a month—in the water with sharks, out where there are crocs, in areas where there are snakes. If we thought it was safe for him, I feel it would be safe for you as well. Just be smart about where you go and who you go with. You will love it.

On a scale of 1 to 10 with 10 being *very* difficult, I give an Australian adventure trip a 3. The only reason it is even as high as a 3 is that the time in the air to get there is long...very long. Aside from that, it is all good and comfortable and a great deal of fun.

#5 Hawai'i

We now live in Hawai'i, but before we did, we visited the islands for fifty-five years or more. You can have a lovely time here as a tourist or conventioneer. Or you can find all the adventures that you can handle.

I advocate for Hawai'i as one of your early retirement trips because it is part of the United States, they speak something close to English, the money is the same, you can find bargain trips if you can put up with a time-share pitch, there's lots of shopping and entertainment on Oahu...and there's lots of adventure on any of the islands.

Lots to do on Oahu...or, as we call it, civilization.

Lots to do on Maui, but smaller and quieter than Oahu. The Lahaina fire sure messed things up, so check carefully before booking a trip. At the time of writing, things are still kind of chaotic.

Kauai gets a lot of attention and is probably our most beautiful island. It is relatively small and the ocean, while beautiful, can be challenging. Be careful out there.

Lanai, Molokai, and the smaller islands are a bit tricky. Lanai is dominated by a couple of beautiful, expensive Four Seasons resorts and not a lot else. Molokai is sparse, so there's not much to do there. It's beautiful but you need to know someone to get to the places that are most beautiful on the island. There are only two gas stations on the island, no franchise fast food places, and not much in the way of hotels so you usually have to book a bed and breakfast or a condo for your stay.

And then there is the best island...the Big Island of Hawai'i. Yes, we live here and are biased as heck. Linda's grandparents lived here going way back. The island has tropical forests, waterfalls, crystal clear ocean, warm water, lots of sea life, good fishing, great golf, volcanoes, every kind of hike, and the world-renowned Lava Light Galleries in Waikoloa Village, which we own with our business partner, CJ Kale.

The island of Hawai'i is bigger in area than all the other islands combined. We have some of the best night skies in the world and a Milky Way season that starts in January, peaks in the summer, and ends in October. Oh...and we have whales and good surf in winter. A favorite big adventure is to go out to swim with manta rays at sunset; it's the thrill of a lifetime. I have been about 500 times and as recently as last night. I never tire of being in the water with those giants of the deep.

You can fly into Kona or Hilo. We suggest Kona. Hilo is beautiful, but it is on the rainy side of the island. Kona is on the drier side.

Come see us (my email is at the back of the book), let me know when you are visiting, and we will do all we can to help you make it a great visit.

On my 1 to 10 scale of adventure difficulty, I give it a 2. It is a bit of a long trip from the mainland of the United States or from anywhere else. Otherwise, it is just plain fantastic. Please do not limit yourself to just Oahu or Maui. Things can be "mo betta," as we say, on the outlying islands.

#4 Yellowstone

I think Yellowstone is one of the most beautiful and interesting places in the world. Every American should try to visit Yellowstone.

I like Yellowstone best in summer when it is warm, all the animals are out, the land looks good, and the vegetation is at its best. However, I honestly cannot stand visiting there in the summer. It's just too crowded, so it's too hard to get hotel reservations and it's too expensive. If you do go in the summer, you will likely end up staying outside the park in West Yellowstone and driving in each day. When we go in summer, we only enter the park at night to do night photography and leave about sunrise before the crowds show up. You might want to bring steady nerves with you if you're going to photograph all night in Yellowstone. There are creatures out there in the night and you will hear them but may not see them until they are right next to you.

We also like to go in the shoulder seasons of spring and fall. There are fewer people around so better accommodations are available. The earlier in the spring and the later in the fall, the better. There will be lots to see but make sure to bring a coat.

This past winter we did something we never thought we would do...went there in the heart of winter. It was minus twenty degrees Fahrenheit every day, with one day hitting minus thirty-six. The first day we saw maybe a dozen people all day; the park was basically empty. The other days we only saw a few snow vehicles like ours. It was an amazing experience and we have already signed up for next winter.

I always feel safe in Yellowstone, but I do keep my eyes and ears open as there are lots of animals around and fabulous scenery. I hope you visit there.

On my travel and adventure scale of difficulty, I give it a 3. It earns that score due to the logistics of working around the crowds and the intricacies of planning your visit. Other than that one caution, I rate it *fabulous.*

#3 Europe

Europe might be a great starter adventure. Pick just about any part of Europe and you will love it. The food is fabulous. I feel very comfortable driving a rental car there. I feel safe, except for when I am out alone late at night. The people are terrific, everywhere, including France. Something to see around every corner.

Where to go? There are lots of tours available and I would advise you to pick one. Great to see London and Paris. Amsterdam is a favorite. I love the South of France, Italy, and Monaco. My favorite spot might be Switzerland...any time of year. And Austria is special, as well.

Look for bargain tours and you will find an outstanding experience at a doable price. A little short on danger maybe, but that can be a good thing.

You will love Europe.

On my difficulty scale, I give it a 3...mostly because they do not have the common courtesy to speak English everywhere, they use funny money, and their electrical system can kill you if you shove a paper clip into it. But you can drink the water anywhere and I would rather eat there than at home. I love Europe.

#2 Peru

I was delighted to find that the Jorge Chavez International Airport in Lima was modern and easy to use. We explored Lima and loved it, but we were careful to heed advice on where NOT to go. We did arrive at the presidential palace during an attempted coup but still managed to get inside the place and meet with government officials...who told us these attempted coups went on all the time. The palace was surrounded by soldiers holding riot shields and standing next to water cannons...quite the sight.

We used only one cab in Lima, and that was only out of dire necessity. Cabs can, according to Peruhop.com, be a problem because Lima is known to have, in their words, "Dodgy, dubious, and dangerous taxi drivers that are unfortunately all too common in Peru. So, you do need to exercise caution, especially when flagging down a cab in the street. All licensed taxis should display some kind of documentation." Have a guide or your hotel arrange your transportation.

Street crime and violence are also common in parts of the city; it's worth finding out where to be especially careful and what neighborhoods to avoid altogether.

We explored the country's coast and were enthralled by that area and the wine-growing region along the central coast. We absolutely loved Lima.

We then traveled to Cusco which is over 11,000 feet above sea level and I had a hard time with it. There are coca leaves legally available for free everywhere to help with altitude sickness. You can drink them as tea or chew them. They contain the coca alkaloids...my wife loved them. Unfortunately, they made me sick as heck—a pounding head and I was unable to sleep.

We encountered two "Hurzeler" signs on our arrival at the Alejandro Velasco Astete International Airport in Cusco. One was being held up by our hired guide. The other was in the hands of a locally known kidnapper. The point being, I try to never get in a car with anyone that I have not fully checked out.

Our guide then informed us that Machu Picchu was closed because there was no way to get to it as the trains were on strike and we did not have time to hike there. No problem, I thought. I had planned for this excursion to take three days. We instead took a bus up the Inca Trail to Machu Picchu and it turned out to be fabulous. The next day we visited Machu Picchu...one of the highlights of our lives. My advice is do not wait until you are really old to go there—it is also at altitude and there are lots of steps, many of them higher than we are used to.

Peru is just plain outstanding, and we left much of it to see in the future. It has some dangers...but, then again, so does downtown San

Francisco. We used guides and hotel staff to keep us aware of hazards and we never felt threatened... except for the one street gunfight that caused us to jump into a forewarned cab to get us out of there. I chose the oldest driver I could find, figuring that if he was going to kidnap us, I might be able to take him in a fair fight. No need...he was perfect.

You could easily do a Peru trip in one week.

I give Peru a 6 on my difficulty scale. Again, they speak some language other than English, their money is weird, and I never did figure out the electrical system. Even an occasional gunfight or attempted coup is off-putting. I am not a big fan of altitude, but that was only a problem in Cusco and Machu Picchu. All that included, I would go back there in a minute. It's one of the most interesting countries I have ever visited, and the people were terrific—except the gunmen and the kidnapper.

#1 Tanzania

You are about to find out why this book was originally titled *The*

Geezer's Guide to Safari. That's the book I was planning to write, but then I decided to expand it to share some thoughts on adventure in general and to describe a few other places on Earth that I consider to be at the top of the list for those with the time and means to travel. You can see by the lick-and-a-promise treatment I gave the first five destinations that I think they are pretty much self-explanatory and easy to figure out. Africa is another story, so I am giving you both barrels of info on Tanzania, which I consider to be *the* most interesting place on the planet.

I am not a safari expert, although Linda and I have been on two exceptional safaris in Tanzania and Kenya. They were highlights of our lives and I am extremely glad that we went on both. However, we went as professional photographers, bent on getting exotic images and making some money from our adventure. So, we pushed too hard, at least too hard for most sane people. Let me explain....

Safari can be an investment of time and money. It can be physically demanding and even dangerous. I will draw from our two major safaris to give you an idea of what I am talking about. **I will then let you know how I think you can do a great safari for much less time and money and in a lot more comfort.**

We live in Kailua-Kona, Hawai'i. To get to Tanzania is roughly a twenty-four-hour plane ride that might take us to Los Angeles, Houston, Amsterdam, and, finally, Arusha, Tanzania. The trip will wear anyone out.

Our last trip to Tanzania, earlier this year, had a major disruption. There was a political problem in Africa that screwed up our plans. So, we flew from Kona to Los Angeles, to Amsterdam, to London, to Addis Ababa, Ethiopia, and then to Arusha, Tanzania. Several people in our traveling party had even more stops. Truth be told, the travel part was exhausting...except we had planned for problems and arrived in pretty good shape.

Since these safaris were designed for professional photographers, they were wonderfully planned and executed. But the days were long, the road travel was rigorous, and the locations were a long way from anything I would call civilization. Overall, the days were tiring and expensive.

When I say expensive, I mean about $50,000 for my wife and me together. Expensive. **I will show you how to go on safari much more economically.**

Comfort? Well, the comfort was top-notch for the conditions, but that does not mean we were comfortable. We did a lot of four-wheel and off-road travel, sometimes at significant speed as we tried to get in position for a "kill" or to see a unique animal that had been spotted. We once hit a warthog den, a good-sized hole in the ground that was covered by the surrounding grass. It was painful! That's because we went from maybe twenty-five miles per hour to zero miles per hour in a nanosecond... and I did not have a seat belt on (don't judge...neither will you) and flew forward head-first into the steel bars of the roll cage. The impact knocked me out...down for the count. When I came to, Linda did the concussion protocol on me, which consisted of asking me if I was ok. I was a bit sore and a bit disoriented...but off we went. After all, we were after a big bunch of lions fighting with hyenas over a lion kill. You don't get to see that every day.

Oh...and there are these things called tsetse flies. They are about the size of a small bird, and they can bite through your pants or shirt. Nasty bastards. They can make you sick as heck, so do your best to fight them off with the zebra tail that the guide gives you. I am not kidding.

Apparently, there are other bugs around. I got extremely sick with the trots and vomiting. It was probably caused by something I ate or drank, but who knows?

We were hundreds of miles out in a vacant area of the Serengeti. There were no structures, villages, or people living on the land for maybe a hundred miles. We had gotten there by a four-wheel drive over land where there were no trails...just animals all around and beautiful terrain, there were no Maasai villages or other civilizations anywhere to be seen.

Plus, my per-day cost was high, and I did not want to miss any part of the safari. But it's kind of hard to be out chasing leopards when you are busy running to the bathroom. I ended up missing half of a safari day and had an extremely miserable night as well. Thank God we had a doctor along; he had the medicine to get me well in a hurry.

On one of the trips, we got caught in the wrong place at the wrong time and had to exit our vehicle and take shelter in a thorn bush—no animal likes a thorn bush. We were caught in a stampede of some 50,000 wildebeests and zebras and our vehicle was on the edge of the cliff overlooking the Mara River. At one point, we thought the animals might push the vehicle over the cliff and into the crocodile-filled river below. We considered that a poor outcome, so we jumped into the thorn bush instead. I mention that to show there can be some danger on safari.

Photo by Linda Hurzeler

And then there are the small planes. You will think I am kidding, but I promise you I am not. We literally had to chase elephants and wildebeests off the short runways to take off in our small planes. By short runways, I mean runways where the small prop planes just barely clear the trees as they lift off. As you read the next paragraph, remember that I am going to tell you how to avoid all this crazy stuff later in the book.

We traveled by air to a small island off the coast of Tanzania...a magical place. However, to get there took us three airplane rides in increasingly smaller aircraft. By the time we took off for the destination island, our plane was only big enough to hold eight people. The pilot...and there was no co-pilot...appeared to be about eighteen years old...seriously. His youth was such that the guy behind me asked if I knew how to fly the plane in case someone had to take over from the kid. I assured him I had thousands of hours as a pilot and could easily step in, as long as the plane used the same software program that I "flew" on my computer, the only piloting I had ever done. The guy did not seem to be amused.

Well, the kid missed the runway. Missed it. He hit it once, then the plane bounced up into the air like we were taking off, and he could not get it back down until we were both long and right off the runway. I was seated directly behind him, listening to the collision alarm blaring and watching the trees in front of us approach at 135 miles per hour as we skipped across the bushes. At the very last minute, he pulled hard on the throttle, adjusted the flaps, and we just barely cleared the trees. It was as close as I have ever come to a very nasty crash. To their credit, the airport emergency crew saw what happened and lined up the runway on our next attempt. I read just last week that that airline, and probably that plane, at that airport, had crashed when the landing gear gave way. I love to fly and love small planes...but, damn, that was close.

What else can I tell you to scare you about safari? I can mention that it is dusty as hell. It can be hot. Cars do break down. We had one break an axle. I was amazed to see the driver patch it up enough to get us to the next tent using some spare parts he had and the roll of duct tape that I always have with me. Cars can get stuck in the mud or while crossing a river, and that could lead to danger. You get the idea—a full-on safari is high adventure.

My guess is that if you go on a standard safari...not the kind I am going to point you toward...you will end up staying most nights in a luxury tent. I know first-hand that the tents are amazing. They have showers with warm water provided by one of the staff pouring buckets of warm water into a holding tank right before you hop in. They have quite nice chemical toilets. Along with great beds with curtains to keep the mosquitos off—you really do not want to get bit by mosquitos in Africa. In addition to electricity and a phone to use if you need help. In each case, we had a very nice tent setup, much like a four-star hotel room.

But let's not overlook the word "tent." Your tent is in an area where there are wild animals...lions and honey badgers to name just two...and potentially snakes. You will be told not to go outside at night without a security person to walk with you. You will be told not to keep *any* food in the room...*any.* Apparently, honey badgers are badass break-in thieves and will sniff out and come after even the one power bar you have squirreled away in your tent.

As luxurious as the tents are, we had a lion kill a zebra and roll into the side of our tent right next to me. He spent the night eating zebra as I lay awake shaking. He then went onto our front deck and availed himself of a bucket of water that should not have been there. I was about three feet away when I peeked out the door and saw his blood-covered face. Of course, I was perfectly safe because there was no way for the lion to get through that one-tenth-of-an-inch-thick tent wall.

There are safari noises...jungle noises. You will not be able to figure out what they are, but they will be way too close, and they will cause you concern. You will not enjoy the night noises. For example, Linda came back to the tent one night after staying in the dining area to talk to a friend. Linda was going to walk the short distance back to our tent by herself—as she claimed that she did not need an escort. However, one of the staff insisted that he accompany her and as he did, he shined his light into the brush. Shining back were at least thirty sets of eyes. That was the night the lion killed the zebra. Lesson learned: We were not on Kona anymore.

Now before I get to the good part, I want to say this: I loved everything I just described. I really never felt in danger...well, maybe a little. We had *excellent* guides and staff, who took care of anything that was a problem. They avoided problems well and did much to keep us safe. The food was adequate to good. I eat such a plain diet on trips overseas that it is unfair of me really to comment on the food, but it appeared to be terrific as I stuck to my bread, power bars, rice, potatoes, and cheese...the "all white" diet. The accommodations were also far better than I had dreamed in such remote locations. What's more, the animals, people, and landscapes that we saw in Africa were the most exciting of my life. We loved both trips.

As of date, we have traveled to 111 countries in our lives. I can say without a doubt that the Tanzania/Kenya safaris were the most interesting trips ever. Just mind-blowing.

However, if you want to go on safari as a professional photographer, staying at least a couple of weeks and visiting the most remote parts of Tanzania and its islands, I am going to give that a score of 8 on my difficulty scale. Why so high? Cost is number one...$50,000 is unaffordable for most people. Keep in mind the price was reduced by our sale of photos from the trip, but not everyone has that opportunity. Plus, it is a long way from home, it requires a lot of planning, and it can be uncomfortable. And while I do not consider it highly dangerous, there is some minor danger. Altogether... an 8.

That said, Linda and I would love for everyone in the world to see Tanzania at least once in their lives. So, we talked about how that trip could be done affordably, take much less time than we took, be safer, and be more comfortable in a way that even people with serious physical challenges could enjoy. We came up with "The Geezer's Guide to Safari." Here it is...

12

The Geezer's Guide to Safari

This is so simple.

The Ngorongoro Crater in Tanzania is one of the most beautiful and animal-diverse places on Earth. It is located just a few hours from the airport you are likely to land at in Tanzania—Kilimanjaro International Airport. You can get to the crater easily and safely by car. You will stay at a luxury lodge... although it too may be a tent, it is not as exposed as the tent resorts in other parts of the Serengeti or elsewhere in Tanzania. The food will be good to great. You will be up on the side of the largest intact volcano caldera on Earth, high enough up that it is cool at night. The volcano is extinct, by the way. The animals that are around are more likely to be elephants than lions. The location is still wild, but much safer than the Serengeti itself.

The crater is one of the wonders of the world and the Ngorongoro Conservation Area is a UNESCO World Heritage site. The crater is large...very large. You can access it via a safe road. The roads inside the crater are dirt roads, but they are mostly flat and well-maintained. You are not driving off across the plains or through streams...you are on decent roads.

You can see, if you are lucky, the big five in the crater—lions, leopards, rhinos, elephants, and African buffalo. You will also see hippos—the most dangerous of all the big animals—the most amazing birds you have ever imagined, monkeys, zebras, hyenas, and on and on. About the only things you will not see are tigers. Tigers live on another continent...try India for tigers. You will also not see gorillas, but you will not see gorillas in the Serengeti either. Try Rwanda or Uganda for gorillas.

On your way into the crater, you will stop at a safe and beautiful place for lunch...and there are several such places...with bathrooms. We even found an ice cream truck. However, you will be in an extremely wild and natural area, with just a few accommodations to make your trip more comfortable. This is not some controlled zoo-like setting—the crater is the real deal.

Also, the real deal is several Maasai villages that welcome visitors. You will find that they want you to buy their goods, but they do not harass you. They seemed genuinely happy that we were there. I found our time in their village to be one of the best parts of the trip.

How many days should you stay? That is up to you. I would suggest three or four. Now there are lots of other parts of Tanzania that I highly recommend, but if you want to do this trip economically, quickly, without getting too far away from modern services—Arusha is a big city with lots of medical and other services available and a great airport to get you out of there in a hurry if you run into a problem—the Ngorongoro Crater is all you need. Fly to Arusha, travel by car or van (I would not go by bus; we saw the bus and you need to trust me on this—do not take the bus) to the Ngorongoro Crater, stay up on the rim in a good lodge, safari three or four days with a great guide, be taken back to the airport, and fly home. You will have had an excellent safari experience—a trip of a lifetime. And you can do it all in about one week, from start to finish from wherever you live.

13

You Need a Guide

You need a guide...and a safari service that will provide that guide. The service will pick you up at the airport, get you to the crater, book you a room, arrange for your meals, hire your drivers and guides, deal with any permits you need or fees you must pay, see to your safety, and help you experience an amazing variety of animals, people, and terrain. All in all, your safari service can make or break your trip.

The main factors that will determine the cost of your trip are....

How many days will your trip be?

What level of luxury do you want for your lodging?

How many people do you want in each vehicle?

A bit about that one...Linda and I are completely spoiled. Our two trips had Land Rovers that could easily fit eight people but carried only three or four—the driver, Linda, and myself, and sometimes a guide in addition to the excellent driver who could also act as our guide.

The fewer people per vehicle the better—and the more it will cost. Four people are OK...five if one is the driver. Six is not nearly as comfortable. We saw things out there that looked like buses. I would rather stay home than be in a vehicle on safari with ten or more people. We saw one vehicle with people fully exposed to the animals as they sat basically in the open on the wheel wells of the vehicle. Don't be one of those people. We saw eight visitors from Japan all standing in a vehicle trying to take photos through the dirt-covered windows. You do not want to be standing all day on safari. Be sure to know how many will be with you in your vehicle. Sometimes a bargain is not a bargain.

If you must trade off amenities to make the trip affordable, choose a better vehicle over better accommodations. Honestly, the trip is about the safari, not the stay. The days are long, and you spend not much more than sleeping time in your rental—whether it's a hotel, tent, or lodge. One caution on the hotel: Make sure it is not a long drive from your hotel to the crater. If it is a two-hour drive, that is four hours of your day spent commuting...not good.

What add-ons do you want?

Add-ons include side trips to other parks, a visit to a Maasai village nearby, a stop at a great place to eat on your way to or from the safari, and a "day room" hotel so you can rest before going to the airport. You can also add on shopping for local arts and things like tanzanite, a beautiful mineral, or a hot air balloon ride. Lots of things to add on if you wish...and they all cost something.

How much will you tip?

Tips are expected and you should budget for them. The safari service will give you a good idea of what to expect, but it can add up to significant money. The fewer days, the fewer tips. And I promise you, you will feel like you have really been on a first-rate safari with just three or four days in the Ngorongoro Crater.

I might add: Whether you are on safari for one day or for thirty, when the last day comes, you will wish you had a few more days. These will have been some of the most memorable days of your life.

What will you buy?

We are seasoned travelers and explorers so we avoid the shopping opportunities. Why? Too much temptation, and sometimes pressure, to buy really great stuff that we do not need. Our grandkids do not need these trinkets. If you want to get something just for the fun of it, you can buy some local stuff at the Maasai villages. They need the money, and their work is really colorful and relatively inexpensive.

14

Know Before You Go

Passports. Make sure your passport is not going to expire for at least six months. If you do not have a passport, or if yours is going to expire in less than six months, I find it worthwhile to pay for expedited service to get one issued or renewed quickly. I carry a photocopy of my passport with me in my luggage or some other place separate from my real one, along with a photo of the important info on my phone. I also carry the passport card with me. It cannot be used as a passport, but it can be a big help in case your passport is somehow lost.

By the way, I always register my travels with the US Department of State. It is a free service. When we were involved in the non-injury plane incident, the State Department and CIA knew about it. It is comforting to know that our government monitors registered citizens when they travel overseas. That could become important should that citizen get caught in a nasty situation like a natural disaster, political chaos, something like a non-injury, or worse, a plane crash. I am all for asking for help from my Uncle Sam if I really need it...and it speeds up that help if the government knows in advance that you are traveling.

Visas. You need a visa to visit Tanzania. I find it easier to purchase it on arrival. Both times I got through customs faster by buying ours at the airport than did the people who bought theirs online. But you may need a visa to stay in other countries where you stop along the way for more than just to change planes so check to find out.

Travel insurance. I am a retired insurance CEO. I think travel insurance is a bit of a rip-off. However, things can get bumpy traveling to Africa, and I suggest you explore or maybe even buy travel insurance for that trip. It could save the day.

What to take? Your safari service will give you a great list. Here are some things I take....

5.11 Tactical® pants...perfect for men and women on safari. There are several styles; the one I currently prefer is Apex. If you are there for just four days or so, you can get by with the pair you wear on the plane and the pair you wear on safari. I love them.

I wear a buff, a scarf made of seamless elastic fabric, to keep flies off me, to protect me from dust, and to cut down on the possibility of sunburn.

A hat keeps the bugs off my head. It's anchored, if you will, by my buff pulled up over the back of my head.

Sunglasses, regular glasses, and a backup pair of each.

A sweater and mid-weight jacket for cool nights and long air travel segments. I carry them on.

The standard amount of underwear and T-shirts, a golf-type shirt or equivalent for the women, regular white socks, and a good set of walking-around shoes. I actually have separate socks and shoes I wear on the plane. Shoes can get really dirty on safari.

Long-sleeve and light-weight shirts. Again, I am trying to not let the bugs get at me. Don't freak out about bugs. It is just that you will run into them from time to time and you do not want them to ruin your day. We also bring mosquito spray with us. There is even soap you can buy to keep mosquitos off.

That's about it for clothing. Pack light. Wear things for more days than you are used to. And most camps have laundry service...so take advantage of it. The lighter you pack the better, but do not expect to stop to buy essential supplies while on safari. Once you leave Arusha and head up the crater there will be no shopping opportunities.

Oh...and you may have to pack some winter clothes if you have a stopover in Europe. Our last trip was in February, so we had some winter clothes for the Amsterdam stop. We put them in the luggage we left at the hotel on the way to safari and picked them up on our way back.

You do not want to be taking bulky stuff with you on safari. Think of one carry-on-sized wheelie piece of luggage and a good-sized backpack. Less is better. Besides, there are no nights at the captain's table with mandatory tux while you are on safari. The people on safari saw me in the same outfit day after day—sometimes freshly cleaned; other days, not so much. They also saw me look worse and worse each day as I chose not to shave for the entire trip. There was at least one guy who looked worse than me, so I felt OK. And, happily for me, he looked really crappy.

Medicine. I am a big fan of bringing my own medicine, especially anything that might fix me up if I get travelers' diarrhea. I am talking about professionally prescribed meds, not OTC stuff. Ask your doctor to prescribe something in case you get sick...you will be *very* thankful you have it if you need it. We take the malaria pills as prescribed. Ask your doctor. For high-altitude locations, make sure to ask your doctor for a prescription that will help prevent the symptoms of altitude sickness.

I do OK at altitude if I have time to acclimatize. On a trip to Peru, we went from sea level to Cusco at 13,000 feet, by plane on a short trip. I immediately felt the altitude...and it got worse. I suffered from headaches and shortness of breath and eventually had problems sleeping. I usually carry an altitude medicine with me, a prescription drug called acetazolamide, but had none for that trip.

The locals suggested I chew the coca leaves to relieve the symptoms. I did so...chewed them and used them in hot tea.

Turns out that coca leaves are the beginning product from which cocaine is manufactured. Unfortunately, I had a bad reaction to the coca leaves...could not sleep at all, was red in the face, my heart was pounding, and my veins stuck out on my face. I wish I had brought along the right meds for the situation...the local remedy just made things worse. On the other hand, Linda loved the leaves and wanted to bring home a suitcase full of them...which turned out to be against federal law and illegal in most states.

The point of this story...know before you go. If you think you might need some help with the altitude, arrange for the right meds for you, oxygen, or a lower altitude place to stay. Altitude sickness is no fun.

Who knows what the COVID-19 situation will be like when you go? Tanzania pretty much stayed open during the pandemic. Your safari operator should tell you what you need if anything.

Money. I only take enough cash for tips and trinkets. I get maybe $500 exchanged for the local currency at the airport. Service people want local currency for tips, and it's good to have a few dollars in local currency for things you might want to purchase along the way. Again, ask your safari people what you should do. Big stores and the like are happy to take credit cards.

Camera gear. I mentioned that my wife and I are professional photographers. Because of that, we look like pack mules when we travel with our camera gear. I hope you do not feel the need to do the same. I think simple is much better...go light. I would get a basic camera or a GoPro and learn to use it properly before you go. I am a big fan of iPhones for video and photos.

If you insist on going big on your camera gear, you will need a minimum of a 400 mm telephoto lens. I shoot with a 600 mm and bring a 1.4 and 2.0 extender with me. I also bring a second camera body with a 70–200 mm lens on it. In my bag, I carry a 16–35 mm wide-angle lens. No tripod is needed. You will be shooting from sandbags resting on the window frame inside your vehicle. You will not be wandering around at night trying to shoot the Milky Way. No filters needed. No remote trigger needed.

But make sure to bring plenty of photo memory cards, batteries, and a charger. I use one memory card a day and carry two batteries with me each day. You will be able to charge the batteries and your phone while in the safari vehicle or back at camp in your room or the lodge.

Bring an electrical converter for Africa…your stuff will not work without it. Check to make sure what electrical equipment works with the converter. Hair dryers and Waterpiks are notorious for burning up with a converter.

I am a professional photographer. I need a laptop computer both to edit my photos on the road and to store my best images. I have also learned to back up those best images…the ones on my camera or phone. It would be no fun to get back home and find your camera or phone is missing and you have no photos for one of the great adventures of your life. I use a 2TB portable drive to store an extra copy of my images. That lets me store one on my laptop and one on my portable drive, and I then always keep the drive with me so that I have the images in two locations. It also allows me to delete those images from my camera card or phone if I need room for new photos. I also back up daily. I have seen people lose several days' worth of photos by not backing up daily. Backing up is a good habit on the road.

That said, doesn't the world have enough images of Africa? If you can just use your phone or something simple, do it. Leave the computer and hard drive at home and avoid the work and cost of the fancy equipment. Then come home and buy some of my photos so I can continue to afford suntan lotion.

I am kind of like a Boy Scout…I am always prepared. I bring along a Swiss Army knife, a small roll of duct tape, tweezers, small scissors, suntan lotion, a flashlight, toilet paper, an eyeglass repair kit, and a magnifying glass. You do not need translator software or an app. You will get along fine without it. If you want to bring along a map or travel guide, you can download it to your phone or iPad. Keep it simple.

I found my phone worked well in Africa. I was able to text, email, and talk for free. But not all carriers work well with Africa's infrastructure, and not all US companies are so generous. You may need to buy a SIM card for your phone in certain countries. You can buy them at the airport. They are easy to use. Your tour guides will tell you if you need them. Internet connections can be sketchy...no real way to know until you get there.

I use Bose headphones or something similar for long flights. I love noise canceling. I suggest you make sure your headphones or earphones have that feature. I fill my iPad with downloaded YouTube clips of old TV shows, podcasts, music, and movies to keep me entertained...I even download a few books.

A favorite book that I have now read dozens of times is ***What's Left of Don***...by me. It is about a two-hour read; you can get it for peanuts as an e-book and the stories will get you laughing and ready for adventure. Plus, you will come away feeling better about your own life, as I have made some pretty stupid decisions in mine and mentioned them in the book. Any proceeds I get from that Amazon best-seller go directly to buy the luxury items that my wife and I have always wanted...so your money is going to a great cause.

That's it for "The Geezer's Guide to Safari" part of the book. To recap....

Fly to Kilimanjaro International Airport.

Have a safari service meet you at the airport and transport you to Ngorongoro Crater to the accommodations they suggest.

Go out on a real safari inside the crater in a safari vehicle with six or fewer people for three or four days.

Have the safari service take you back to Kilimanjaro International Airport and fly home.

I think you can do the whole seven-day trip with no add-ons or upgrades for about $4,000 a person...maybe lower if you can catch some great airfare deals. Additional days are about $500 to $1,000 a day per person. A business-class upgrade to and from Tanzania could add another $2,000 per person or more (certainly much more if you do not follow my advice to work with a consolidator). And if you decide to go for a full-on week or two safari to the wildest places in Tanzania, with lots of add-ons, then I wasn't kidding about the $50,000 price tag. But keep in mind that our trips are tax-deductible and that we sell images (hey...and maybe books) from these trips.

15

Some Concluding Thoughts on Becoming Adventuresome in Your Senior Years

When my dad died at ninety-four, I had the task of going through his things and settling his estate. No fun, and I am betting most of you have been through something similar. My dad led an amazing life. He left home at eighteen, joined the US Army Signal Corps, and served in Europe during World War II. That service brought him ashore on D-Day plus three and marched him across the continent and into Germany. He then had a nearly fifty-year career that ended when he turned seventy, having served as head of quality control for the B-2 stealth bomber, and worked in top secrecy for the last ten years of his career.

I mention his background to talk about what I found when he passed. His employer had given him a packet of information on the things he needed to know for retirement. Every photo in it was of someone doing something like knitting or relaxing in a rocking chair or sitting in a crappy-looking boat in a crappy-looking lake, fishing for crappies. You could not find one suggestion of a vigorous or adventuresome life anywhere in that retirement packet. I wish I had kept it, but it pissed me off so much I threw it away.

We become what we think we will become. We envision a sedentary, boring retirement because those around us, society, and the press tell us how to think. To be fair, we also think that way because of what we observe on our own.

The killer of fun in old age is us—our own minds, our own thoughts. It is not some set of instructions sent down by God that you must follow. Our fun in old age is up to us, and no one else can create it for us.

"Your journey is completely yours. It is unique. Others may try to steal part of it, tell it in their words or shape it to suit them. Reality is no one can live it or own it but you. Take charge of your journey, it's yours and yours alone!"

—Kemi Sogunle

16

Finding Fun in Our Senior Years

My thoughts on the years I have left....

I am going to use this miracle of retirement to accomplish as many of my dreams as I possibly can.

I am going to push my limits, get out of my comfort zone, try and fail, try and succeed, pivot and try something else...until I am happy and leading a vigorous and adventure-filled life.

I am going to do none of the above foolishly. I will work hard for my success, but rest as often and long as needed as I make progress, get help from experts to speed up my progress, seek their honest feedback on my progress, ask them to help me do things safely, and to watch out for my safety.

I now take naps. I did not know naps existed until I retired. I am now a major league proponent of naps.

I couldn't care less about looking awkward along the way. You are reading the words of a guy who got full metal braces on his teeth at age seventy-two. I don't care about failing along the way, but I would like to accomplish my goals in the end. And if I find that some goals are not possible to achieve, I will pivot and try something else. When I do that pivot, I will not think of that as failure...more like, "What's next?"

I have the time to go back and try to recapture the joy of things I did in my youth, like surfing or snorkeling. This is a great time to try to find your old guitar or paintbrush. And heck yes, I always wanted to see the world and I am going to find a way to make that happen.

I may not sound like it, but I am a realist. I know things like health issues, the health status of those closest to us (perhaps our spouse), their mobility, and our finances can impact what we can and cannot do in retirement. We all have to deal with reality. But I want to challenge some of that reality.

17

What Stops Us from Turning Dreams into Reality?

What stops us can certainly be reality. If you are fighting cancer right now, you are not going to pack up and take a big trip to Egypt or anywhere else. If you are fighting to pay the rent, you are not able to pursue some activities you'd otherwise like to. If your wife is in a wheelchair, you are not taking the two of you mountain climbing. Reality sometimes sucks, but it is what it is, and we all do our best to deal with it.

But here is a killer of dreams that IS NOT reality. It is your obligations in retirement that keep you from making your own dreams come true.

I had a multimillionaire cousin who gained his wealth late in life. He was a member of Rotary and attended Rotary meetings every single week for something like fifty years. Rotary has a rule of eighty-five that allows a person whose combined age and years in Rotary equal eighty-five or more to skip meetings if they wish. He did not take advantage of that rule.

My cousin used his newfound wealth to fly from the United States to Paris, saying he always wanted to see the world. He left on

Thursday and returned on the following Tuesday, so he could attend his Rotary meeting. He found the travel so difficult in that short time frame that I am not sure if he ever traveled again.

I do not fault him for his loyalty to Rotary; in fact, I am proud of him for that loyalty. I do wish he had found it within himself to explore the many new possibilities available to him when he gained his freedom and could retire due to his newly acquired wealth. Instead, he settled for his long-standing routine. As a result, I think he missed the opportunity of a lifetime. But I am not my cousin, and it was his choice. What will your choice be...continue as is or find out what adventure may brighten and enrich your life?

I retired after over forty years in the insurance business. I had some success. I had some skills. I certainly could have continued to this day hanging onto that profession and the connection with a lot of people I love and like in that community. And I don't think it would have been horrible had I done so—there would have been some enjoyment there and probably some good money.

Instead, I made a big decision at age sixty-one. I decided to retire and find out what else I had in me. I purposefully went after the things I had dreamed of doing all my life—becoming a small business owner, learning photography, traveling the world, investing my time, knowledge, and money in people I cared about, writing books, and helping others write their books and get them published. At the same time, I wanted to limit my efforts so that I had time to really goof off, become sloppy, a bit unreliable, and do what I wanted when I wanted.

That was my decision. I of course made sure it fit the wants and needs of my wife of over fifty-five years first, and, yes, she signed up for the same program. We are now business partners, photo partners, travel partners, writing partners, and co-incompetents when it comes to knowing the day of the week. It has made for the best time of our lives.

Do not take this for me thinking poorly of my cousin or anyone who has basically not changed their lives at all in their retirement years. People make their own decisions and agree with them or not, I respect those decisions. I just want to challenge them a bit to take one more shot at maximizing their chances to do all they really want to do in life.

I want to challenge that word, **obligation.**

YOU make up the obligation. It is an invention of **your** mind. Sometimes that invention is something someone taught you. Sometimes it is a guilt trip someone put on you to meet their own needs...not yours. Sometimes it is a guilt trip you put on yourself for some perceived past failing. Sometimes it is something you invented to protect yourself from having to change. Whatever it is...it is not chiseled in stone or written in some US federal law. It is just something you have come to believe is true. You can change it. There is no change fee; it is free, just like your own free will.

I have written often about being a bit selfish at certain points in your life. I never find the right words to make me look like a wonderful person when I suggest that I do certain things selfishly...but I do them anyway.

That's because I believe I have only one life. I understand that I am now on the other side of the average lifespan of American males. I also know that half the people I grew up with are now dead. That number gets bigger each year. One day, my turn will come.

I ask you to believe the following without question, and I promise that it is in large part true. I have led a generous life. I am still living it. I have gone out of my way to help those around me. I have given up my time and resources for the benefit of others regularly. I served, led, and helped finance many charities. I helped people...still do. I would bet you fit into the above description too.

I added those two last paragraphs together and made a purposeful decision: I am going to use what little time I have left to take care of my wife and me and to make sure we get to do what we have always wanted to do. That means I will not be the go-to driver to take the kids to baseball practice. I will not always be there to take someone to the doctor. I will not live just down the street from someone I love in an area that does not jive with my lifestyle just out of obligation or expectation that I do so. Won't do it. Selfish? Yes...on purpose. And I feel good about it.

I will...be there when needed, be present in meaningful ways, stay in contact, help when I can, and accumulate some resources so that when I pass, I can make things easier for future generations of Hurzelers and others.

But damn it, I will not live my life out of some made-up obligation.

Obligations. I am obligated to pay taxes and follow the law...and the set of morals that I adhere to. That is the full list.

And you?

"He needed to get away from the rush of the city, from the unceasing noise and annoying obligations."

—Francine Rivers

You can do anything your mind lets you do. You are fully in charge of your own decisions.

Obligations are constraints you put on yourself. I challenge each one of you with the thought that NOW is your time to get what YOU want. The obligations may now have to be put aside so you can turn your dreams into reality.

I AM HERE TO LISTEN AND REPLY TO YOUR THOUGHTS, COMPLAINTS, OR QUESTIONS

Got questions or want to discuss anything in the book? Contact me at djhzz@aol.com. I would love to hear from you. I wish you the biggest and best retirement that you could ever imagine. And thank you for spending this time with me.

"Don't let your dreams be dreams."
—Jack Johnson

Aloha.

Don Hurzeler Bio

At the time he wrote this book, Don was seventy-seven...an official geezer. He and his wife of fifty-five years, Linda, have traveled to 111 countries so far. These days, they are professional photographers by trade, but the fact is, they are really retired and just having fun with their cameras.

Don was an NCAA Division II All-American sprinter and hurdler. He had a forty-plus-year business career that included being CEO of an insurance company and national president of The Society of Chartered Property and Casualty Underwriters. Don earned an AA degree in insurance and a BA degree in business and economics. He also did postgraduate work at Harvard and Northwestern's Kellogg School of Management. He holds the Chartered Property and Casualty Underwriters (CPCU) and Chartered Life Underwriters (CLU) insurance certifications.

Don currently serves on the board of directors of the Ends of the Earth Conservation Fund and is a member of the Ocean Artists Society. He won the Nature's Best Photography: Windland Smith Rice International Award for nature's best photography, along with many other awards for photography. He also won the Axiom Business Book Awards' gold medal for his book *The Way Up: How to Keep Your Career Moving in the Right Direction*.

Don and Linda, along with their business partner, CJ Kale, own Lava Light Galleries, Inc., a fine art landscape photography gallery and business in Waikoloa Village, Hawai'i. Don owns Kua Bay Publishing LLC, and has written eight books. Check him out at donhurzeler.com.

Acknowledgments

I want to acknowledge Thomson Safaris, *Nature's Best Photography* magazine and Steve Freligh, the African Wildlife Foundation and Craig Sholley, and Todd Gustafson of Gustafson Photo Safaris for helping me to fall in love with Africa.

I am appreciative of the world's airlines, cruise ships, and travel agents for getting me to exotic places and back.

Big thanks to my business partner and friend CJ Kale for teaching me to be a photographer—along with Nick Selway...another fantastic photographer—and for keeping me semi-safe on the lava, in the mountains, and in the ocean.

Thanks to my adventure hero, Eli Martinez of *Shark Diver Magazine* and Shark Diver Excursions for keeping me alive when you might not have thought that would be possible while swimming with saltwater crocodiles and other large animals...in places I would never have visited on my own.

I also appreciate having the big, strong Chris Knight of London at my side in some interesting situations.

I want to specifically thank United Airlines for years and millions of miles of great travel...and the Marriott and Hilton Hotels & Resorts for always having a great room for us.

I cannot get books out the door without the help of Charles Levin, Steve Bennett, and Tanya Hayes Lee...thank you.

A big thanks to the owner, captain, and crew of the Kona-based, ocean-adventure boat, *Sunlight on Water*, who have kept me safe in unsafe situations and have helped me to really push my envelope on ocean adventures.

Same thanks to Deron Verbeck, Brett LeMaster, and Wild

Hawai'i Ocean Adventures for getting me semi-comfortable in the deepest part of the ocean with just a camera in my hand confronting whatever we might find.

And special thanks to our grandkids for letting us show them what adventure looks like, here and around the world.

Big thanks to Pike Thompson for his photo of me in the water at sunset.

And then there is Linda...my wife...who has saved me from a shark attack, kept me from being run over by careless boat captains in Australia and Dominica, and put up with my outrageous schemes like, "Honey, how would you like to go to Egypt right before a revolution? I have arranged for armed security for the whole trip." "Let's go," she said. Quite the partner for adventure.

Thanks also to Linda for her photos in this book. The rest of the photos were taken by me, with one other exception.

Special thanks to our grandson Nathan Stanczak for his photo of the clown fish taken on the Great Barrier Reef.

Last and most importantly...thank *you* for taking the time to read my book. I hope you enjoyed it. Aloha.

*To learn more about Don and his other books, view his
photographs from around the world, or contact him,
visit donhurzeler.com*

9 789898 587559